C000228904

The CRAFTY HANDS *Collection*

Creative Candles
Face Painting & Fancy Dress
Marbling
Perfect Parties
Rag Dolls
Salt Dough Models
Simple Projects in Patchwork

First published in English in Great Britain
1996 by Aurum Press Ltd,
25 Bedford Avenue, London WC1B 3AT

English translation copyright © Aurum Press 1996

First published as
Peinture sur Soie
1996 by Éditions Fleurus,
11 rue Duguay-Trouin, 75006 Paris, France

Copyright © Éditions Fleurus 1996

All rights reserved.
No part of this publication may be reproduced or utilized
in any form or by any means, electronic or mechanical,
including photocopying, recording or by any information storage
and retrieval system, without prior permission in writing from
Aurum Press Ltd.

A catalogue record for this book is available from the British Library

ISBN 1 85410 441 1

1 3 5 7 9 10 8 6 4 2
1996 1998 2000 1999 1997

Printed in Italy by G. Canale & C. S.p.A. - Borgaro T.se - TURIN

The CRAFTY HANDS Collection

SILK PAINTING

Text and illustrations by
Eva Dimcovski
Photographs by Dominique Santrot

Aurum Press

■ *The Magic of Silk*

Silk, that magical, fascinating fabric, synonymous with luxury, richness and taste, is endlessly adaptable to colours and designs. Silk painting requires just a few basic supplies, and it's something anyone can do — even the youngest. This book is full of ideas for presents to make and decorate from plain white silk — scarves, cushion covers, greeting cards, tunics, purses — all brilliantly coloured and painted with ease.

We give thirty simple projects, grouped by themes — the sea, animals, flowers, Christmas, Africa — but you can use your imagination to create many more, and as you get bolder, you will discover the scintillating effects of gold and silver gutta, the kaleidoscopic salt technique, how to paint a watercolour picture. Combine projects by mixing colours and techniques. Be brave and experiment — and good luck!

MATERIALS

Silk

Although silk comes in many different weights and qualities, not all of them are suitable for silk painting. We used a white silk pongée (No. 9 thickness). It is smooth and shiny and holds colour well.

Silk Paints

Silk painting dyes are either water-based or spirit-based. Water-based paints can be thinned with water to lighten the colours, and are usually made permanent or 'fixed' by ironing on the wrong side. Some can be fixed by applying a liquid fixer. Spirit-based paints are fixed by steaming. Although the fixing process is more complicated, the results give clear, brilliant colours. But whatever paints you use, read the manufacturer's instructions carefully, and fix as recommended.

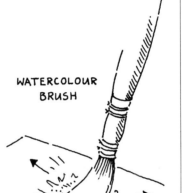

WATERCOLOUR BRUSH

PAINT

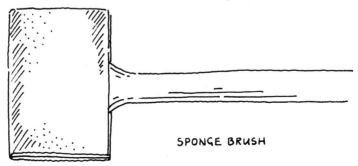

SPONGE BRUSH

Brushes

You will need two types of brush — fine ones for detail and thick ones (or a sponge-brush) for large areas. Watercolour brushes are good, as are Chinese paintbrushes.

A Frame

To work on the silk you will need to stretch it over a frame. Although it's easy to make one, you can get them ready-made, in sizes up to 90cm/36in square, with notches allowing you to adjust for smaller pieces of silk. Keep your frame clean by covering the sides with masking tape for each session.

Diluting/Thinning Agent

Because it can be difficult to spread colour evenly across large backgrounds, a commercially prepared thinner added to spirit-based paint helps to give a nice, even texture. It also lightens the colour. Depending on the paint you are working with, water can also be used. Around 10% of either should be adequate. Check the manufacturer's instructions.

You will need: Graph and tracing paper; soft pencil; masking tape; silk pins; small containers; absorbent paper; white spirit; coarse salt.

Mosaic scarf, page 12.

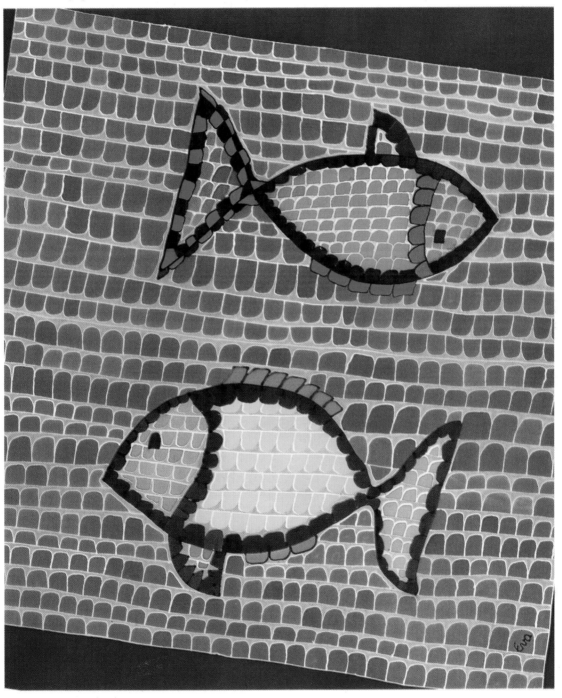

■ *Techniques*

Resist Technique

This is sometimes called gutta technique, serti technique or blocking technique, as the outline of the design is blocked in with gutta resist, which prevents the colours from running into one another. The serti is also decorative. Before painting, hold the silk up to the light to check that the lines are solid and the outlines closed – the colours run only too readily!

Blocking with gold gutta.

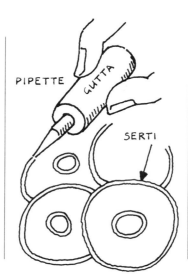

Gutta Resist

Gutta Resist is a thick liquid that penetrates the fibre of the silk to create a barrier that prevents the colour from spreading. Clear or transparent gutta is water-soluble, so when you wash your silk painting, the resist is removed along with any excess paint and liquid fixer, and the original colour will show. Resist also comes in colours, or in gold or silver. These are not water-soluble, so any details drawn using them will remain in your design.

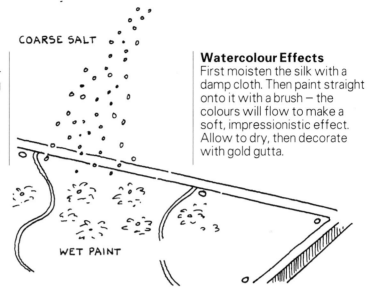

Salt Technique
Sprinkle salt over freshly painted silk. It will create interesting
marbled effects – coarse salt
will produce large-scale
effects, finer salt will give a
more subtle veining. This easy
technique is useful for background colours (see page 19).

COARSE SALT

WET PAINT

Watercolour Effects
First moisten the silk with a
damp cloth. Then paint straight
onto it with a brush – the
colours will flow to make a
soft, impressionistic effect.
Allow to dry, then decorate
with gold gutta.

Salt effects for the background.

Watercolour background.

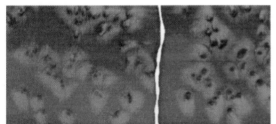

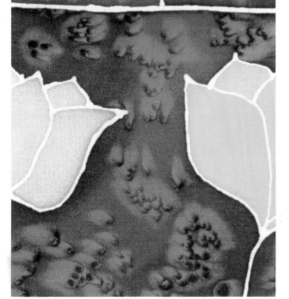

■ *A Few Words of Advice*

Drawing Motifs
We have given you the principal motifs for our designs. Copy them onto squared paper, then reduce or enlarge them according to the shape of your project. Tape your drawing onto the table, fix the silk over it, and lightly trace the drawing onto the silk with a soft pencil.

Working on the Silk
Attach the silk to your frame with silk pins. It should be stretched tightly and evenly and pinned every 8–10 cm (3-4in), to create a taut, flat work surface. Make sure the silk does not touch the table.

Applying the Gutta
Fit the gutta bottle with a suitable nozzle or transfer the gutta to a dispenser. Press gently to start it flowing, then draw the outline of your design with rapid, even strokes. Wipe any drips from the nozzle with absorbent paper before each new start. Practise first on a scrap of silk.

Painting a Background
Spread the colour as fast as possible to avoid watermarks. Get others to help you: each starting at a different corner and working fast to finish all together in the centre. If you are working alone, go over the background several times, or use a special diluent to help even colouration.

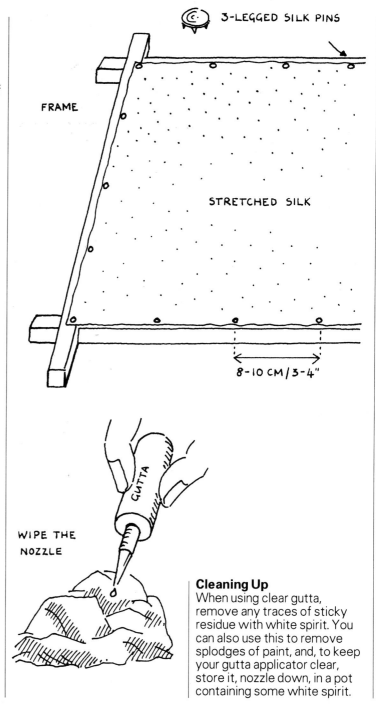

3-LEGGED SILK PINS

FRAME

STRETCHED SILK

8-10 CM / 3-4"

GUTTA

WIPE THE NOZZLE

Cleaning Up
When using clear gutta, remove any traces of sticky residue with white spirit. You can also use this to remove splodges of paint, and, to keep your gutta applicator clear, store it, nozzle down, in a pot containing some white spirit.

■ *Finishing Touches*

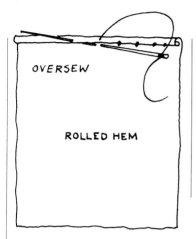

OVERSEW

ROLLED HEM

Scarves, Ties and Purses
Rolled hems give the best finish. They should be sewn by hand. Of course, if you are impatient, you can always use the sewing machine!

Cushion Covers
Fix, wash and iron the silk. Cut backing fabric (you can use plain or matching silk) to size, and place both pieces right sides together and machine stitch the layers around three sides. Press seams flat. Turn right sides outward. Insert a cushion pad, then oversew the remaining opening to close.

MAKING-UP A CUSHION

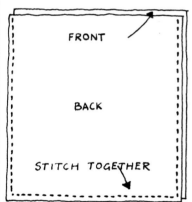

FRONT

BACK

STITCH TOGETHER

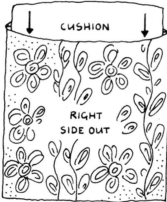

CUSHION

RIGHT
SIDE OUT

Making Cards
When making cards, maximise your efforts by painting several little designs on the silk at the same time. Fix, wash and iron the silk, then cut out each piece. Place them on self-adhesive paper, smoothing with the heel of your hand to press out air bubbles and creases. Cut around your designs with pinking shears, then glue each to a piece of card.

Careful finishing is indispensable in order that your silk creations retain their charm and elegance.

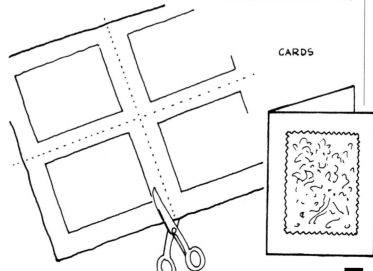

CARDS

■ *Finishing Touches*

Tunics

Take a length of silk 180 x 90cm/72 x 36in and fold to make a 90cm/36in square. Do not cut it. Attach to the frame and copy the design shown, front and back, then fix it, wash and iron. Cut out the tunic following our pattern (allowing 2.5cm/1in seams all round). Machine the sides and the shoulders, press the seams flat, then hem raw edges.

Lavender Sachets

Cut two squares and sew up three sides, as for a cushion cover. Turn right sides out, fill with dried lavender and oversew to close. Tie with a ribbon.

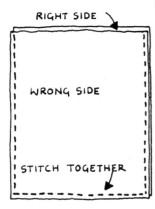

RIGHT SIDE

WRONG SIDE

STITCH TOGETHER

FRONT

CENTRE

BACK

Fish for T-shirt (see page 16).

■ *All the Fish in the Sea*

MOSAIC SCARF

You will need: 90 x 90cm/36 x 36in silk pongée; black and clear gutta; diluting agent.
Colours: lemon yellow; rust; navy blue; royal blue; light blue; red; pink; black.

Preparation

Using graph paper, square up and enlarge our design, to give a fish 40cm/16in long. Trace it onto a sheet of paper of the same size as our scarf. Reverse your design to trace the other fish below. Trace a border 10cm/4in from each edge, then trace horizontal lines every 2–3cm/³/₄in–1¹/₂in across the paper, using these lines to draw the scales and the waves. Copy your design onto the silk and fix it to your frame.

Colouring:

Outline the fish with black gutta, then define the scales, the frame and the waves with clear gutta. Allow to dry. Fill in the eyes and the outer scales with black, the rest of the scales with bright colours. Paint the background in royal blue (diluted), the waves in light blue and the border in navy blue. Allow to dry. Fix, wash and iron, then hem the edges.

Photo on page 5.

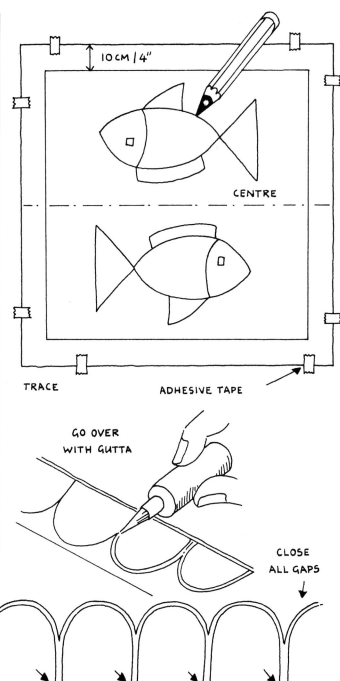

10CM / 4"

CENTRE

TRACE

ADHESIVE TAPE

GO OVER WITH GUTTA

CLOSE ALL GAPS

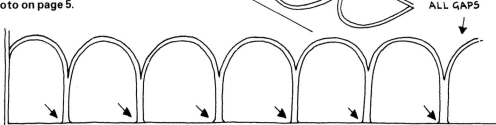

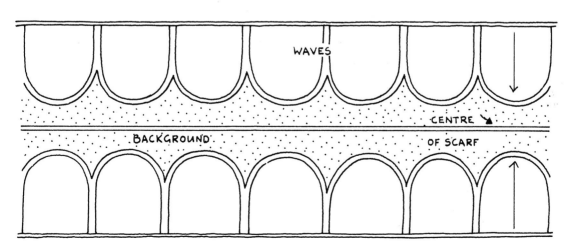

WAVES

CENTRE OF SCARF

BACKGROUND

■ *All the Fish in the Sea*

DEEP BLUE SEA-SCARF

You will need: 90 x 90cm/36 x 36in silk pongeé; clear gutta; diluting agent.
Colours: apple green; jade green; moss green; prussian blue; ultramarine; navy blue; gold yellow; orange; sand; fuchsia; deep violet; coral.

Preparation
On a sheet of tracing paper, draw a wavy border about 15cm/6in from the edge. Draw a circle of fish in the centre – copy ours, or use your imagination. You could have octopus, crab, starfish, sea horses. Surround the motifs with seaweed and branching coral. Transfer the design to the silk, attach it to your frame and block it out with the gutta. Hold to the light to check that the gutta has sunk in properly, leaving no gaps. If in doubt, go over it again, and leave to dry.

Colouring
Using a fine paintbrush, paint in some of the coral in red and orange, others with a mixture of red and diluted brown. Use the greens for the seaweed. Use your imagination to colour the fish, taking care the colours go well together. For the border, mix navy blue and jade green and dilute slightly. Dilute this mixture further for the background. Fix, wash, then iron while damp between two sheets of absorbent paper. Hem the edges.

DRAW THE BORDER

BACKGROUND

Deep blue sea-scarf. Lavender sachet (see pages 10/18).

■ *All the Fish in the Sea*

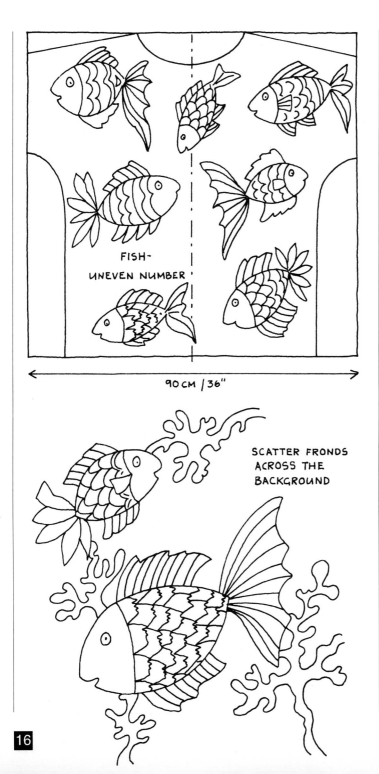

FISH-
UNEVEN NUMBER

← 90 CM / 36" →

SCATTER FRONDS
ACROSS THE
BACKGROUND

FISH FOR T-SHIRT

You will need: enough silk to make a square 90 x 90cm/36 x 36in; clear and blue gutta resist; diluting agent; tracing paper.
Colours: yellow; orange; light blue; royal blue; turquoise; ultramarine; apple green; moss green; brown; raw umber; burnt sienna; fuchsia; pale pink; black.

Preparation
Trace the outline of our T-shirt onto graph paper, and enlarge to your size. Draw in the fish, the corals and the seaweed and transfer to the front of the silk. You can either repeat the design on the back or simply leave it blank. Attach to your frame. Block out the fish in blue gutta; use clear gutta for the scales, the coral and the seaweed. Allow to dry.

Colouring and Finishing
Paint the background first; dampen the silk, then dilute the apple green, royal blue and navy blue colours and paint on with a thick watercolour brush. Use rapid strokes, allowing the colours to flow together and beyond the borders of the pattern.
Then paint the fish, using clear bright colours for some, diluting or mixing the colours for others. Highlight the fins by outlining with fine lines of blue gutta.
You can repeat the pattern on the back, or simply paint it in the background colour all over. Allow to dry. Fix, wash and iron. Cut out the T-shirt according to our pattern (allowing 2.5cm/1in seams all around). See page 10 for making-up.

■ *Bright Colours*

MULTICOLOURED SCARF

You will need: 1.2m x 55cm/ 60 x 22in of silk pongeé 9; black gutta resist; coarse salt; diluting agent; tracing paper.
Colours: light yellow; deep yellow; bright green; red; violet; bright blue; navy blue.

Design and Serti
Draw wavy lines all over your tracing paper. Work freely and don't worry about the effect. Transfer to the silk, using a soft pencil. Attach to the frame. Make sure that it is quite taut – put newspapers beneath, too, as the salt will weigh down the silk. Block out your design with the gutta, as shown on pages 6 and 8. Check that it has sunk in properly. Allow to dry.

Colouring
Measure about 20 drops of each colour into containers. Lighten some tones by adding 6 or 7 drops of diluting agent, if you wish. Paint some of the motifs with pure colour, others with the diluted colours.

Working with Salt
While the silk is still damp, sprinkle with salt and leave to dry (see page 7). Shake off surplus salt and remove the residue with a soft brush. Fix as recommended by the manufacturer, wash and iron, then roll the hem of your scarf.

LAVENDER SACHET (illustrated on page 15)
Draw circles using black or gold gutta resist. Paint them and fill in the background in bright colours. Fix, wash, iron, then make up as shown on page 10.

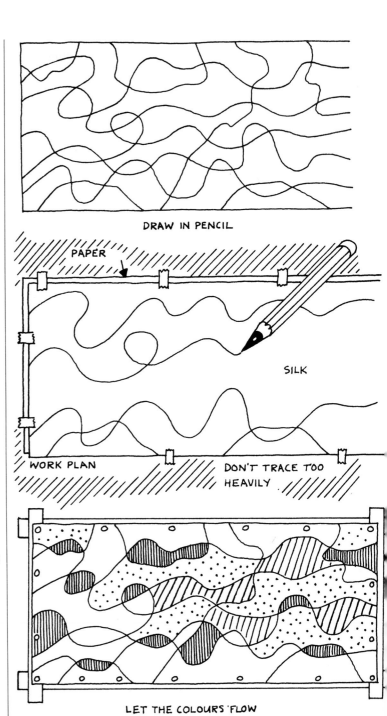

DRAW IN PENCIL

PAPER

SILK

WORK PLAN

DON'T TRACE TOO HEAVILY

LET THE COLOURS FLOW

Multicoloured scarf. Harlequin cushion (see page 20).

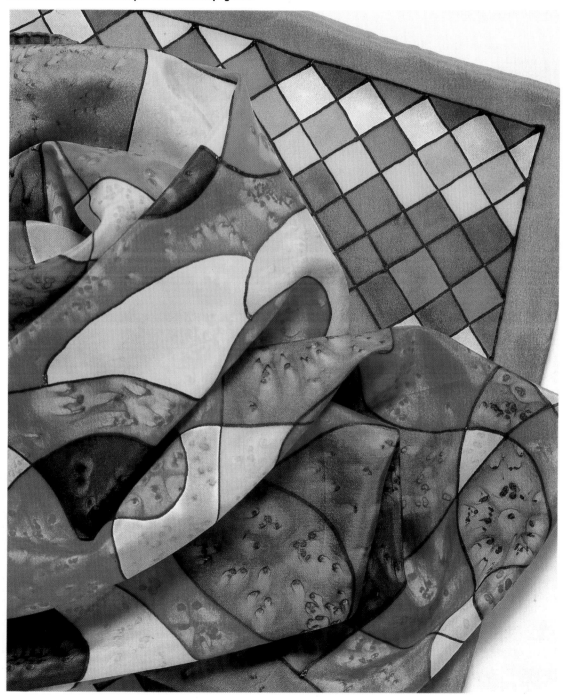

■ *Bright Colours*

HARLEQUIN CUSHION

You will need: 45 x 45cm/
18 x 18in of silk plus backing
fabric; cushion pad; black gutta
resist.
Colours: yellow; sage green;
fuchsia; royal blue; navy blue;
light blue.

Preparation:
On a sheet of tracing paper,
draw a 39cm/15in square.
Starting from the corners,
mark it off in 3cm/1¼ in seg-
ments. Draw diagonal lines
then parallel lines to each point,
as shown. Tape the paper to
your worktable and secure the
silk to it. Trace the design onto
the silk in pencil. Protect your
frame with masking tape and
stretch the silk tightly over it,
attaching with silk pins.

Blocking

If necessary, decant the gutta
resist into an applicator bottle
with a fine nozzle. Now trace it
over the lines you have previ-
ously traced onto the silk. As
you begin each new pass, take
care to wipe the drip of gutta
that will form at the tip of your
nozzle. Check that all lines are
solid, then allow to dry.

Painting and Finishing

Arrange the colours by rows: a
horizontal line of navy blue, a
vertical line of light blue; a horizontal line of fuchsia; a vertical
yellow one, etc. Finish with a
fuchsia border. Allow to dry.
Fix, wash and iron, then make
up as shown on page 9.

Illustrated on page 19.

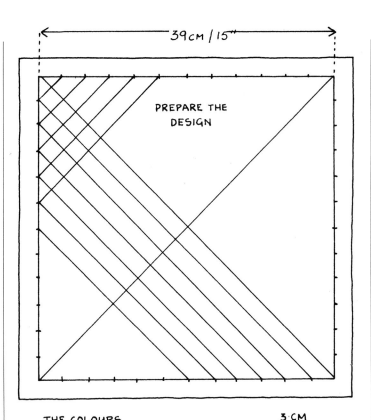

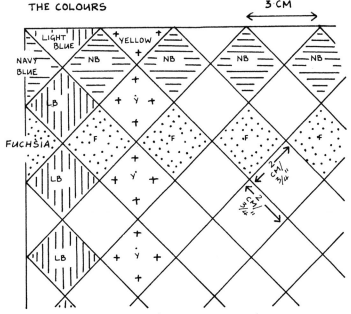

■ *African Impressions*

CROC-O-CUSHION

You will need: 45 x 45cm/18 x 18in of silk and suitable backing; cushion pad; black gutta resist; diluting agent.
Colours: dark green; bright green; moss green; brown; cobalt blue; light blue; black.

Cushion photographed on page 23.

Enlarge the motif (the whole crocodile and the head) and trace it onto the silk. Outline with black gutta, and draw in eyes, teeth and nose, too. Colour the heads by dabbing with the dark and bright green. Use the same method for the backgrounds, diluting the light blue and the cobalt blue, the brown and the moss green. Dampen the surface of the silk, so that the colours will mix and flow gently into one another, and work rapidly. Allow to dry, fix, wash and iron. Make up as shown on page 9.

■ *African Impressions*

CAMEL'S HUMP

You will need: 45 x 45cm/18 x 18in of silk and backing fabric; cushion pad; black gutta resist; diluting agent.
Colours: royal blue; prussian blue; light brown; flesh pink; gold yellow; black.

Enlarge the motif and trace it onto the silk. Attach it to the frame and outline with gutta, adding the line of the dunes. Use brown slightly diluted for the dunes and paint the camel with a mixture of brown and flesh pink. Mix and dilute the two blues for the sky. Detail the eye, the toenails, and the tail in black. Allow to dry. Fix, wash and iron. Make up .

Camel cushion. Quilted tortoise, page 26.
Croc-o-cushion, page 21. Pink elephants, page 25.

■ *African Impressions*

Post a giraffe on a tunic.

GIRAFFE STAMP TOP

You will need: 180 x 90cm/72 x 36in of silk; black gutta resist; diluting agent.
Colours: yellow; violet; light blue; bright green; light brown; black.

Draw the pattern of the top (front and back, see page 10) onto squared paper, and enlarge it to your size. Transfer to the silk. Enlarge the giraffe motif and trace it onto the front. Attach the silk to your frame. Block in the design with black gutta. Allow to dry. Colour it in: begin with the giraffe and end with the blue sky. Paint a black line around the stamp and block in the background colour – a diluted mixture of yellow and brown. Allow to dry. Fix, wash and iron the silk. Cut out the top and assemble.

PINK ELEPHANTS

You will need: 45 x 45cm/18 x 18in silk and backing fabric; cushion pad; black gutta resist; diluting agent.
Colours: rose pink; navy blue.

Copy the elephant motif onto tracing paper and draw three rows of two or three elephants onto the silk. Paint the top row pink. Dilute the colour slightly for the middle row, and again for the bottom row. For the background, use undiluted blue for the bottom row, then dilute slightly more each time for each of the succeeding rows. Allow to dry. Fix, wash and iron. Make up into a cushion cover, as shown on page 9.

Full design shown on page 23.

■ *Family Pets*

QUILTED TORTOISE

You will need: a black silk top; 20 x 15cm/8 x 6in of silk and wadding; assorted small beads; black gutta resist; diluting agent.

Colours: yellow; light blue; bright green; moss green; light brown.

The design
Trace off the motif and transfer to the silk. Attach to the frame and draw in with black gutta, then colour in the rest of the tortoise, as shown. For the background, mix and dilute the moss green and light brown. Allow to dry. Fix, wash and iron.

Quilting
Fix the silk to the wadding by sewing green beads onto and through the green areas, yellow beads on the yellow areas, etc. Appliqué the motif to the front of a black silk top, turning in the edges about 5mm/¼in all around.

Photographed on page 23.

MIDNIGHT PROWLER

You will need: 40cm/16in silk; black gutta resist; diluting agent.
Colours: gold yellow; orange; brown; midnight blue.

Preparation and Painting

Enlarge the cat motif, adding the brick wall and the moon. Trace onto one end of the silk and reverse to trace onto the other end. Attach to the frame, outline with gutta and allow to dry. (You may need to leave one end hanging loose, if your frame is not long enough). Paint the bricks in yellow and orange. Add a dash of brown, and dab in with a soft brush. Reverse the silk and paint in the other motif. Then fix the silk in your frame so that the white space for the background is held firmly in the centre. Dilute the blue and paint in the sky rapidly. Fix as necessary, wash and iron.

KITTY CUSHION

You will need: 45 x 45cm/18 x 18in of silk and backing fabric; cushion pad; black gutta resist; diluting agent.
Colours: gold yellow; orange; brown; midnight blue.

Proceed as for the scarf, but enlarge the design to have only one cat in the centre of the cushion. Colour the cat in brown, the moon in yellow, and the bricks as for the scarf.

Making up

Fix, wash and iron under absorbent paper. Make up the cushion cover and roll the hem of the scarf.

■ *Family Pets*

FLOPPY PUPPY SCARF AND CUSHION

You will need: 90 x 90cm/36 x 36in of silk for the scarf; 45cm/18in of silk and backing fabric for the cushion; cushion pad; black gutta resist; diluting agent.
Colours: red; black; brown; rust; yellow; beige.

Preparation and Painting
Enlarge the motif to suit your project, and modify it as you wish (bow, direction of the tail, etc). Trace it four times onto the scarf, 25cm/10in from each corner, with all tails going towards the centre. Draw lines between the puppies to make a frame. You could make several different cushions, by varying the size, the positioning and number of the puppies, or by simply using the heads. Attach the silk to your frame. Block the outlines with the gutta and allow to dry. Mix brown and beige to shade in the bodies; deepen the effect by adding some black. Paint the bows yellow or red, the eyes and whiskers black, the rug beige and the background rust. The heads, the paws and the tip of the tails are left white.

Finishing
Fix as necessary, wash, then iron. Make up the cushion and scarf as shown on page 9.

A naughty little puppy to paint on scarves and cushions.

■ *Season of Silk*

CHRISTMAS CUSHION

You will need: 45cm/18in of silk, plus backing fabric; foam cushion pad 40cm/16in square; black gutta resist; diluting agent.
Colours: gold yellow; orange; royal blue; light blue; moss green; bright green; dark green; russet brown; beige; brilliant red; black.

Copy the sleigh motif and square up to the dimensions of your cushion. Trace onto the silk, and mark off the line of the horizon to divide the background. Attach to your frame, and outline in gutta. Allow to dry. Colour the stars and the moon in yellow, the sledge in yellow and royal blue, with the runners in russet brown and beige. Colour the hearts in red. Use the greens for the pine trees. Dilute royal blue for the sky, and dilute russet to wash over the ground. Add touches of black, as shown, to the trees and the sleigh. Allow to dry. Fix as necessary, wash and iron. Make up as shown on page 9.

CHRISTMAS STOCKING PURSE

You will need: 30 x 30cm/12 x 12in of silk; black gutta resist; diluting agent.
Colours: as above

Using a soft pencil, trace the design of the stocking in a corner of the silk. Attach to your frame and block in with the gutta resist. Allow to dry, then paint in the motif. You can make it stand out by outlining the design in brown, softening it by dabbing with red to fade into the background,which is coloured with diluted red. Fix as necessary, wash and iron. Cut out, leaving 2.5cm/1in seam all round,and cut another stocking shape from the red background. Make up as shown on page 9 or 10. Sew a zip at the top.

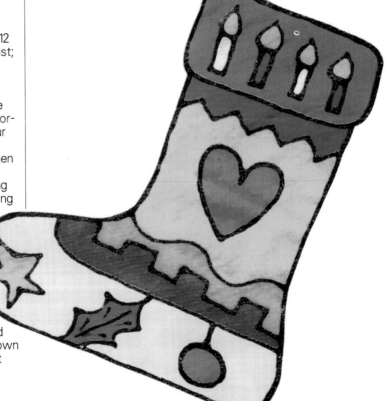

Christmas cushion.

■ *Season of Silk*

NOËL NOËL

You will need: 90 x 90cm/36 x 36in silk; black and gold gutta resist; diluting agent.
Colours: gold yellow; orange; apple green; bright green; dark green; jade green; royal blue; prussian blue; violet; brilliant red; black.

Preparation
Copy different Christmas motifs onto a sheet of tracing paper, using those from pages 30–35 to inspire you. Position them according to the plan on this page, then trace in pencil onto the silk and stretch it on your frame. Block the outlines with black gutta, making sure all lines are closed. Allow to dry.

The Colour Scheme
Colour the pines and the holly by mixing the greens. Leave little circles for snowballs and wavy spaces for layers of snow. Use red for the holly berries, the heart and the sugar stick, and outline with black. Use yellow for the candles and other motifs. The candlelight is done by first painting a circle of yellow, then an outer circle of orange, allowing them to flow together slightly. See our pictures for other touches. Then paint in the centre of the garland and the background. To speed up the drying, you could use a hair-dryer, working from the sides into the centre, being careful not to hold it too close to the silk. Finally, decorate with touches of gold gutta. Fix as recommended, wash and iron. Finish by hand-rolling the hems.

■ *Season of Silk*

CHRISTMAS WINDOW

You will need: 45 x 45cm/ 18 x 18in silk and backing fabric; foam pad; black gutta resist.
Colours: red; gold yellow; brown; royal blue; almond green; russet.

Draw directly onto the silk . The border is 3cm/1in from the edges, the window frame about 4.5cm/2in from the border. Draw the bricks and the window panels. Draw the decorations and run zigzag lines between them. Then fix to your frame and block in with resist; allow to dry, then colour. For each brick, dab a little russet in the corner, then dilute to finish in a lighter colour. The background is a mixture of gold yellow, russet and brown. Fix as required, wash and iron. Make up as shown on page 9.

CHRISTMAS CARDS

You will need: scraps of silk (15 x 10cm/6 x 4in per card); backing paper; gutta resist in clear, black and gold; thin card to fold into envelopes.
Colours: red; gold yellow; brown; royal blue; almond green; violet; orange.

If possible, paint several designs on the same piece of silk (see page 9). Attach it to your frame and draw freehand in the gutta. Use black gutta for the outlines and transparent gutta for the snowflakes. Allow to dry, then paint. Dot some gold gutta over parts of your design. Fix, wash and iron. Cut out and glue to card.

SNOWY NIGHT CUSHION

You will need: 45 x 45cm/ 18 x 18in silk and backing fabric; foam pad; black and gold gutta.
Colours: yellow; dark green; beige; brown; royal blue.

Using a soft pencil, copy the pine trees, alone or in little groups, onto the silk. Add the moon and the mountains. Fix to your frame and block with the black gutta. Allow to dry. Colour the pines with green and beige, the moon in yellow, the sky with a mixture of the two blues, slightly diluted. Make the shadows on the snow with touches of brown and beige, then take a clean brush and wash over them with clear water. Allow to dry. Add dots of gold gutta to the pines. Fix, wash and iron. Make up as on page 9.

Snowy night cushion.

■ *Gilding Effects*

RED AND BROWN GILDED SCARF

You will need: 90 x 90cm/36 x 36in of silk; diluting agent; gold gutta; 5 real dried leaves. **Colours:** gold yellow; red; brown.

The Background
Protect your table with newspaper and a sheet of plastic. Prepare the colours in little jars. The red is used undiluted. Add a drop of brown to the yellow, then dilute. Fold the silk square in half and fold again, to make four thicknesses. Paint the folded corner yellow, continue painting outward with red, and finish with brown, as shown in the illustration. Unfold the silk and allow to dry.

Printing the Leaves
Coat one of the leaves, on the veined 'wrong' side, with gold gutta. Put it gutta side down on the silk, cover with blotting paper and press. Remove the leaf and repeat with fresh leaves. Remove, and allow to dry. Fix as necessary, then wash and iron on the reverse. Hand roll the hem, as on page 9.

GREEN SCARF

Dampen the silk (see page 7) and paint with slightly diluted green and yellow, using a soft, thick watercolour brush. Begin in a corner and work rapidly to avoid water marks. Print the leaves and finish as shown above.

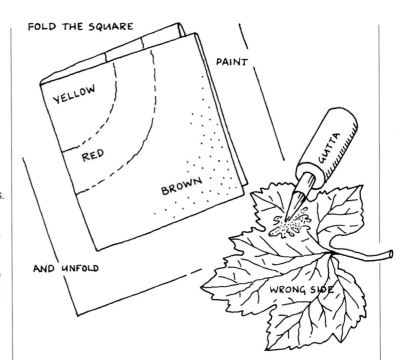

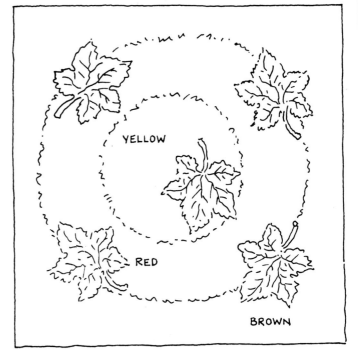

■ *Flowered Silks*

LADYBIRD, LADYBIRD

You will need: 45 x 45cm/18 x 18in of silk and backing fabric; foam cushion pad; gutta resist in black and blue; diluting agent. **Colours:** orange; bright green; moss green; gold yellow; light yellow; brown; royal blue; black.

Trace the design, then fix the silk to your frame. Block the outline of the flowers in blue gutta and that of the ladybird in black. Allow to dry. Mix the two yellows for the heart of the flowers. Paint the tips of the petals in red and fill in with diluted yellow. The leaves are moss green, with veins in black gutta. The ladybird's spots and her head are moss green, with a dab of blue for the eyes. Fix, wash and iron. Make up as shown on page 9.

FLORAL CUSHION

You will need: 45 x 45cm/18 x 18in silk and backing fabric; cushion pad; gutta resist in gold and silver; diluting agent. **Colours: red;** bright green; moss green; gold yellow; lemon yellow; brown; royal blue; black.

Copy the different flower motifs and trace them several times onto the silk, in order to make a circle of flowers. Affix to your frame, then block the outlines with gold or silver gutta. Allow to dry.
Paint in the flowers as you please, or follow our colour scheme. Fix as required, wash and iron on the reverse side. Make up the cushion as shown on page 9.

Cushion cover with yellow, pink and blue flowers.

■ *Flowered Silks*

TULIP TIME

You will need: 90 x 90cm/36 x 36in of silk (or 45 x 45cm/18 x 18in of silk and backing fabric suitable for a cushion cover; gutta resist in silver; diluting agent.
Colours: lemon yellow; orange; pink; royal blue; moss green; bright green.

Using the picture on the right, draw some tulips on tracing paper; transfer them repeatedly onto the silk, placing them as shown. First do the flowers around the centre, then fill in round the edges. Fix the silk to your frame and block the outlines with silver gutta. Allow to dry. Paint the stalks and leaves with diluted moss green, the tulips in lively colours, the background in bright green. Add dashes of orange in the grass to create shadows, softening the edges with a brush dipped in clear water. Fix as required, wash, iron and make up.

A FRIEZE OF FANTASY FLOWERS

You will need: Silk; clear gutta resist; coarse salt; diluting agent.
Colours: light blue; lemon yellow; bright green; dark green; pink.

Fix the silk to your frame. Draw the flowers in the clear gutta. Paint them yellow, blue and pink. Allow to dry. Using the water-colour technique (see page 7) paint the background in bright and dark green. Sprinkle the salt over the damp silk, allow to dry (see page 7). Fix, wash and iron. Make up.

A frieze of fantasy flowers to make a cushion, a scarf, a tie.

A border of tulips for a scarf or a cushion.

■ *Flowered Silks*

ROSES AND VIOLETS

You will need: 45 x 45cm/18 x 18in silk and backing fabric suitable for a cushion; foam pad; clear or silver gutta resist; diluting agent.
Colours: purple; fuchsia; blue; lemon yellow; dark green.

Using a soft pencil, draw the large flowers directly onto the silk in rows; fill in the gaps with little flowers. Pin to the frame and block the outlines with clear gutta. Don't forget the centres and the little rays, as shown. Allow to dry. Paint the hearts, the petals then the background. Fix, wash and iron. Make up as on page 9.

BLACK CUSHION

You will need: 45 x 45cm/18 x 18in silk and backing fabric; foam pad; gutta resist in gold and silver; glitter paint; diluting agent.
Colours: royal blue; prussian blue; violet; gold yellow; bright green; pink; black.

The Design
Draw the motifs in pencil on the silk, working in rows for the different shapes. Fix to your frame, then block the outlines with gutta or glitter paint. Make sure there are no gaps. Allow to dry.

The Colours
Colour in the flowers and the leaves as shown. Paint the background black, starting with the smaller spaces, then fill in to the border. Allow to dry overnight, then fix as necessary, ironing on the reverse side. Make up as on page 9.

Black cushion.

■ *Flowered Silks*

BLUE FLOWERED CUSHION

You will need: 45 x 45cm/18 x18in silk and backing fabric; foam cushion pad; clear gutta resist; diluting agent.
Colours: red; gold yellow; blue; brown; russet.

Trace the flowers and transfer to your silk. Affix to the frame and block the design with clear gutta. Allow to dry. Colour the large flowers blue; dab the colour on the tips of the petals, then wash over it with the dilutant, using a soft, thick brush. To give depth, draw light blue lines with a fine brush. Paint the rest of the flowers and allow to dry. Fix as required, wash and iron between two sheets of absorbent paper. Assemble the silk and the lining as shown on page 9.

GREEN BACKGROUND

You will need: 45 x 45cm/18 x18in silk and backing fabric; foam cushion pad; diluting agent; black gutta resist.
Colours: bright green; gold yellow; orange; pink; light blue; deep blue.

Trace or draw the flowers onto the silk – large ones first, filling in the gaps with little ones. Fix to your frame and block the outlines with black gutta. Allow to dry. Paint the flowers as shown. Fill in the large flowers in yellow, then add a touch of orange to the tips of the petals, blending it in with your brush. Fix as required, wash and iron. Make up as shown on page 9.

They all came up!

■ *Flowered Silks*

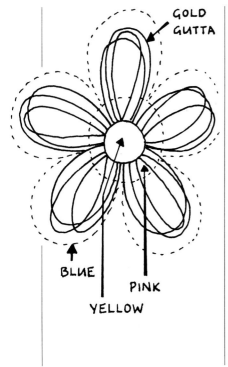

GOLD
GUTTA

BLUE

PINK

YELLOW

TAPESTRY CUSHION

You will need: 45 x 45cm/ 18 x 18in silk and backing fabric; cushion pad; diluting agent; gutta resist in gold.
Colours: bright green; moss green; light blue; navy blue; pink; gold yellow.

Dampen the silk with a sponge (see page 7). Fix it to your frame and paint a band of diluted light blue down the left side. Paint a moss green stem with leaves in bright green. Add a line of little yellow circles and a ruffle of rose pink. Paint navy blue petals around this. Paint another green stem, and continue on with a new band of blue, a green stem, a column of flowers and another blue band. Outline the petals and the stems with gold gutta. Allow to dry. Fix as required, wash, iron and make up as shown on page 9.

BANDS OF FLOWERS

You will need: 45 x 45cm/18 x 18in silk and backing fabric; clear gutta resist; diluting agent.
Colours: deep blue; royal blue; green; lemon yellow.

Draw the flowers as shown. Alternate with a line of wavy ribbon in deep blue. Pin to your frame and block the outlines with clear gutta. Dilute the deep blue to lighten it and paint strips of progressively lighter blue, leaving one white strip. Paint the petals by mixing the two blues, diluting the colours to give depth and contrast. Paint the leaves in green and the centres in yellow. Fix as necessary, wash and iron. Make up as shown on page 9.

■ *Contents*

■ *Product Information*

Most craft shops stock a range of silk painting dyes and accessories. Some names to look for:

Steam-fixed dyes:

Dupont, Elbesoie, Knaizeff; Pebéo, SilkArt.

Iron-fixed dyes:

Deka, SetaSilk, Marabu, Elbetex.

Stockists:

Specialist Crafts Ltd., PO Box 247, Leicester LE1 9QS.
Telephone: 0116 251 0405. Fax: 0116 251 5015.
Suppliers of art and craft materials, also available through Reeves/Dryad shops.

Silk Painting Centre, Nobles Barn, Blendworth, Horndean, Hants PO8 OAH.